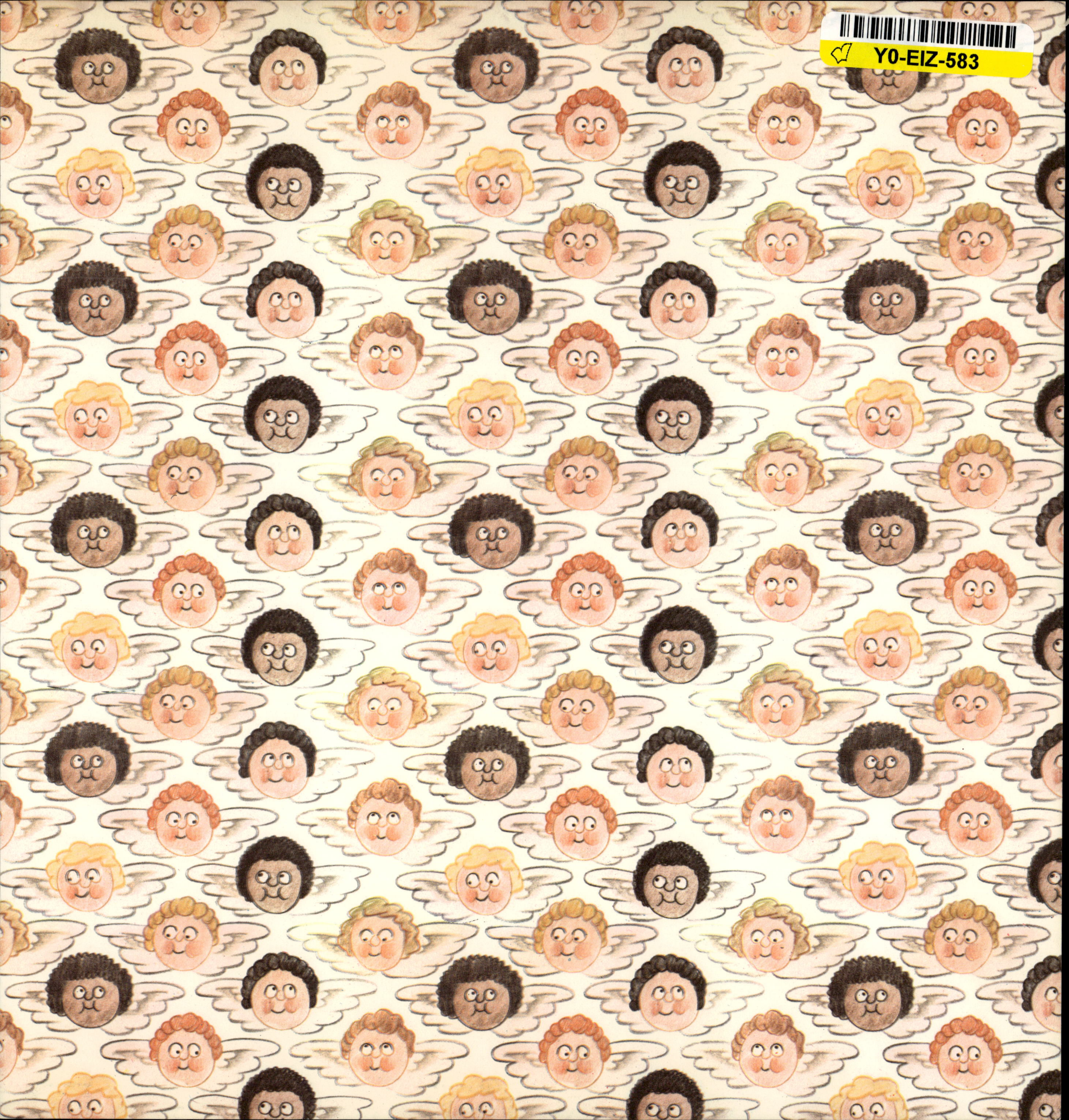

Donna

"WILL I GO TO HEAVEN?"

by Peter Mayle

CORWIN BOOKS

NEW YORK

For Courtney, with best wishes for a happy life.

Second Printing, 1976

Copyright © 1976 by Peter Mayle
Library of Congress Card No. 76-1190
ISBN 0-498-01983-7

All rights reserved. No part of this book may be reproduced in any form without permission in writing from Corwin Books except by a newspaper or magazine reviewer who wishes to quote brief passages in connection with a review.

Manufactured in the United States of America

Published by

CORWIN BOOKS
275 MADISON AVENUE
NEW YORK, N.Y. 10016

People have said that Heaven is like one long Christmas Day. People have said that Heaven is where you never have to go to bed. People have said that Heaven is just the other side of the clouds in the sky.

In fact, people have been talking about what Heaven is like and where it is for hundreds and thousands of years. But the truth is that nobody really knows.

That's because nobody has ever been there and come back.

Heaven is not like any place on earth. You can't go and visit. You can't send letters telling your friends what the weather is like and how you're getting along. You can't make phone calls (not even Long Distance). And you can't come back home for weekends. No, once you go to Heaven, that's where you stay.

It may not sound like much fun, being stuck in one place all the time. And yet, for all these thousands of years, Heaven is where people have wanted to go. So there must be something very special about it.

In this book, we're going to try to tell you a little about what we think Heaven is like. But because we've never been there, we're going to have to use our imaginations. You'll have to use yours, too. Maybe between us, we'll get an idea of what it is that makes Heaven such a great place.

We'll start with one of the very few things we know for sure about Heaven: you can't get there while you're living on earth. Heaven is somewhere you go *after* your time on earth. In other words, you can't get to Heaven before you die.

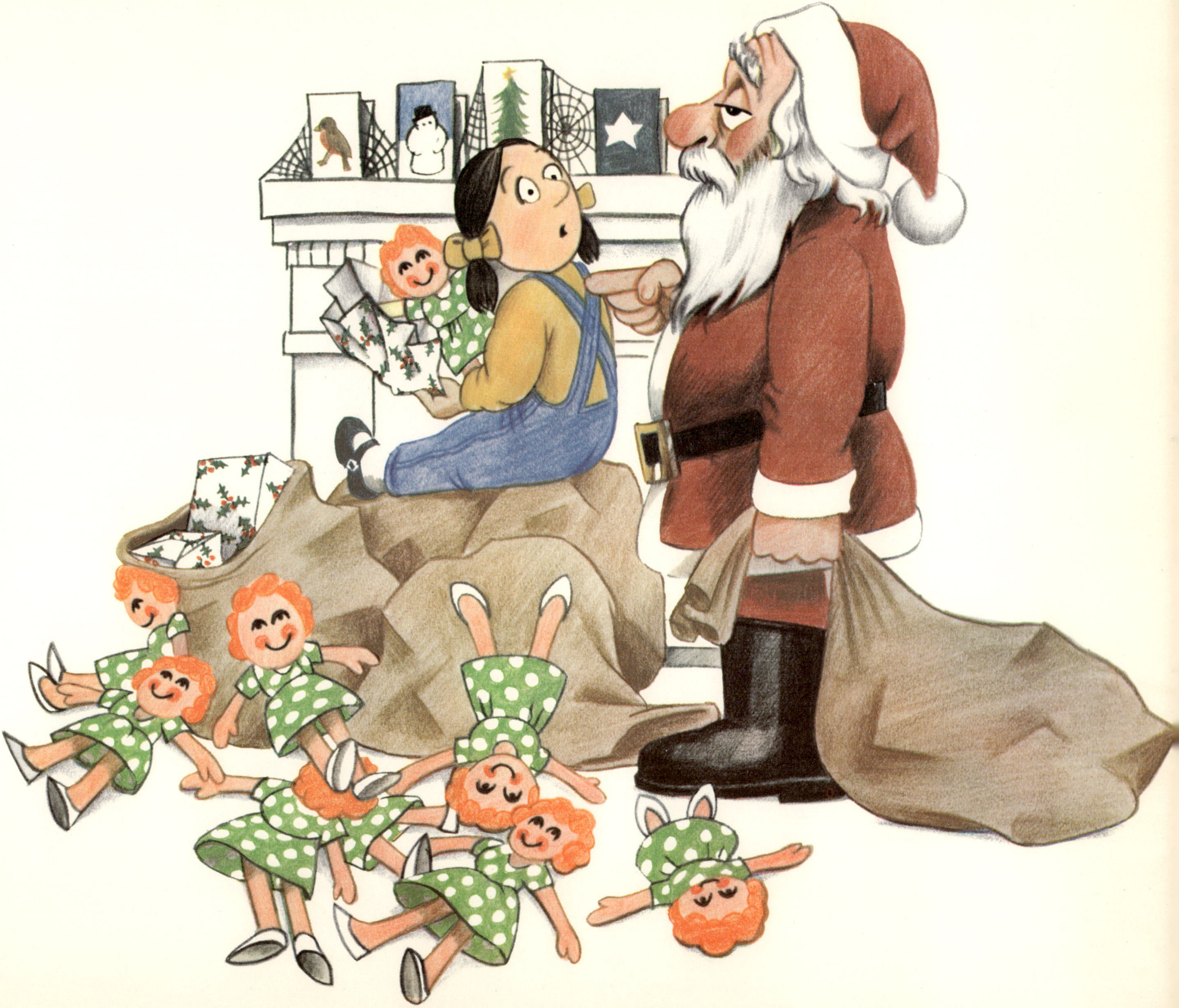

WHY DO WE DIE?

Nobody likes the thought of dying. It means the end of life, which is something we know about. And the beginning of death, which is something we don't know much about. And unknown things are often scary.

Sooner or later, though, we all die. And not just people. Every animal, every flower, every tree—they all have only a certain length of time on earth.

This lifetime can be very short, or very long. A butterfly, for instance, only lives for a few hours. Trees often live for hundreds of years.

People come somewhere in between. The longest life a person has ever been officially known to have is 113 years. But living that long is very unusual.

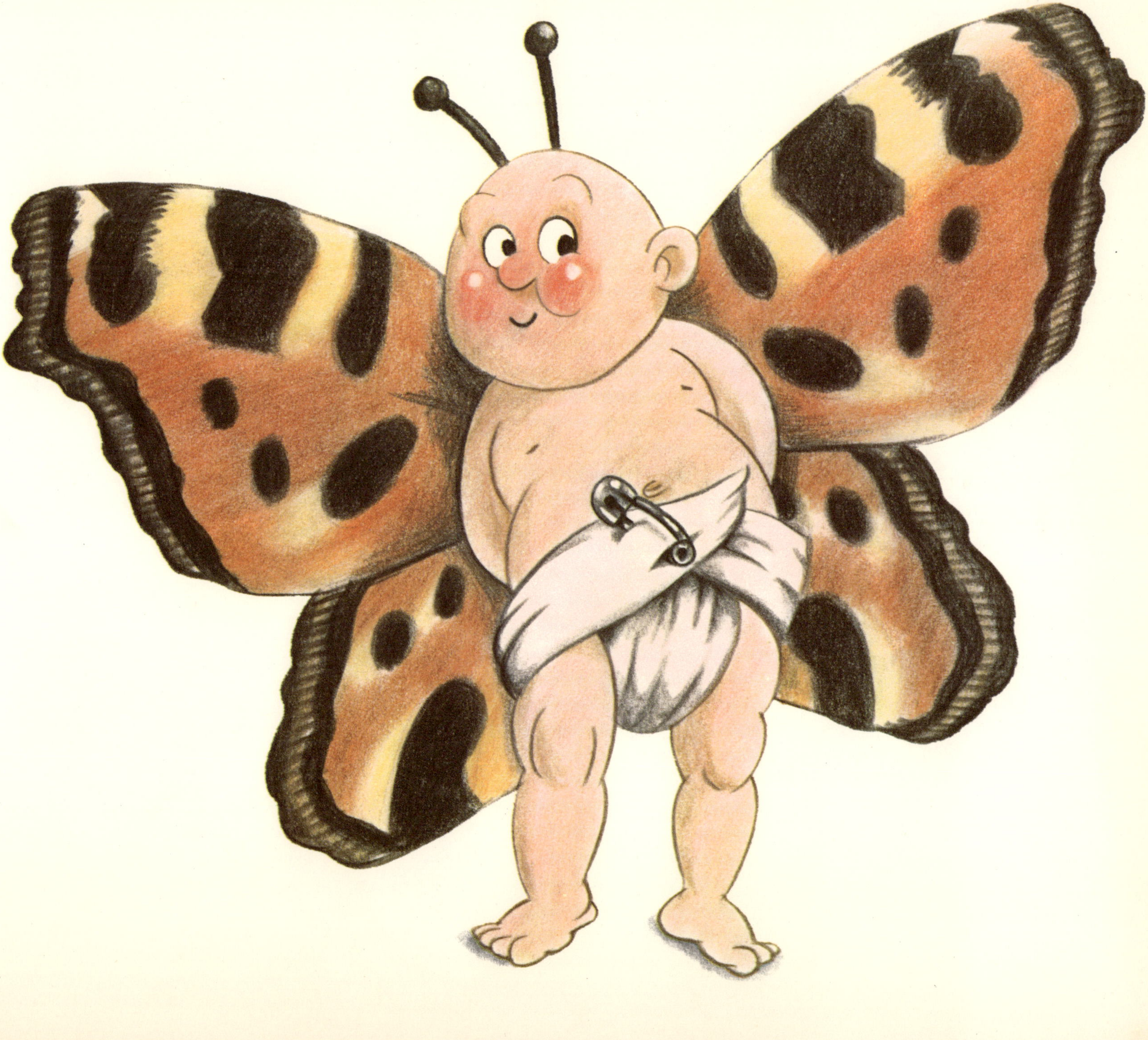

If we're lucky, most of us can expect a life of about 70 years, which is certainly a good long time.

And during those years, we do what every other living thing does. We're born. We grow up. We grow old.

Then comes a time, after maybe 60 years or 70 years or 90 years, when we get so old we just wear out. What happens is that your heart, which is what keeps your body going (rather like the engine of a car or the battery of a radio) gets tired and stops working. And when that happens, you're dead.

Dying is sad, and it's no use pretending it isn't. After all, when someone you like or someone you love dies, it means you won't be seeing them again on earth.

But just because you won't be seeing them every day like you used to, it doesn't mean they don't exist any more.

They've simply gone some place else. Or at least, part of them has.

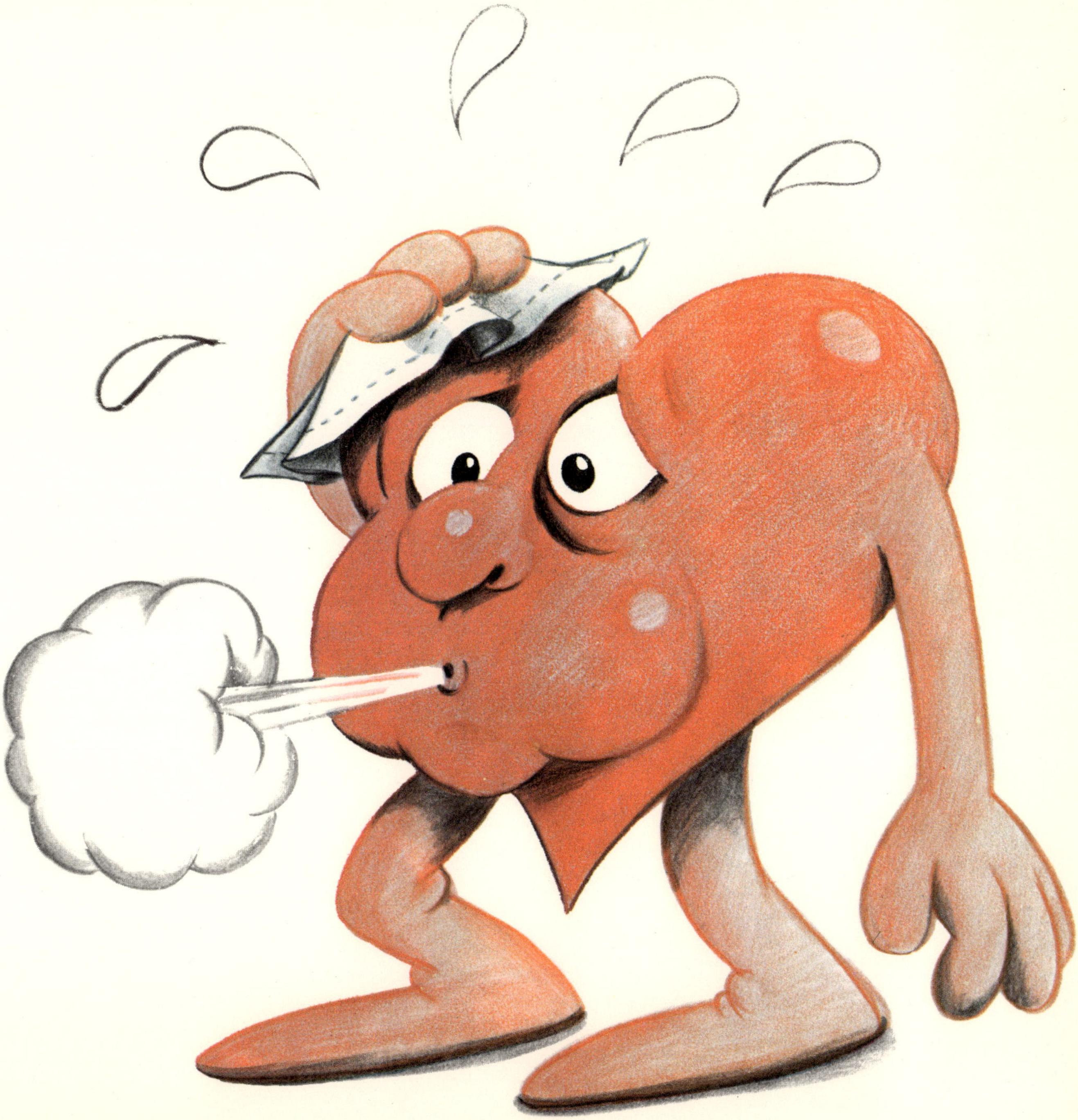

WHAT HAPPENS AFTER WE DIE?

This is where you're going to have to start using your imagination, because this is where it becomes quite difficult to understand.

Before you can understand properly, you need to know about the difference between your body and something else that's even more important—your soul.

Your body, as you know, is made up of things you can see, or touch, or feel: your head, arms, legs and so on, as well as all the inside parts of you, like your heart and tonsils.

Your soul is inside you, too. But it's not something you can see or touch.

It is the non-body part of you, and it is the part that really decides what kind of person you are. If you're kind and gentle, that's because of your soul; not because you have brown eyes or black hair or long legs.

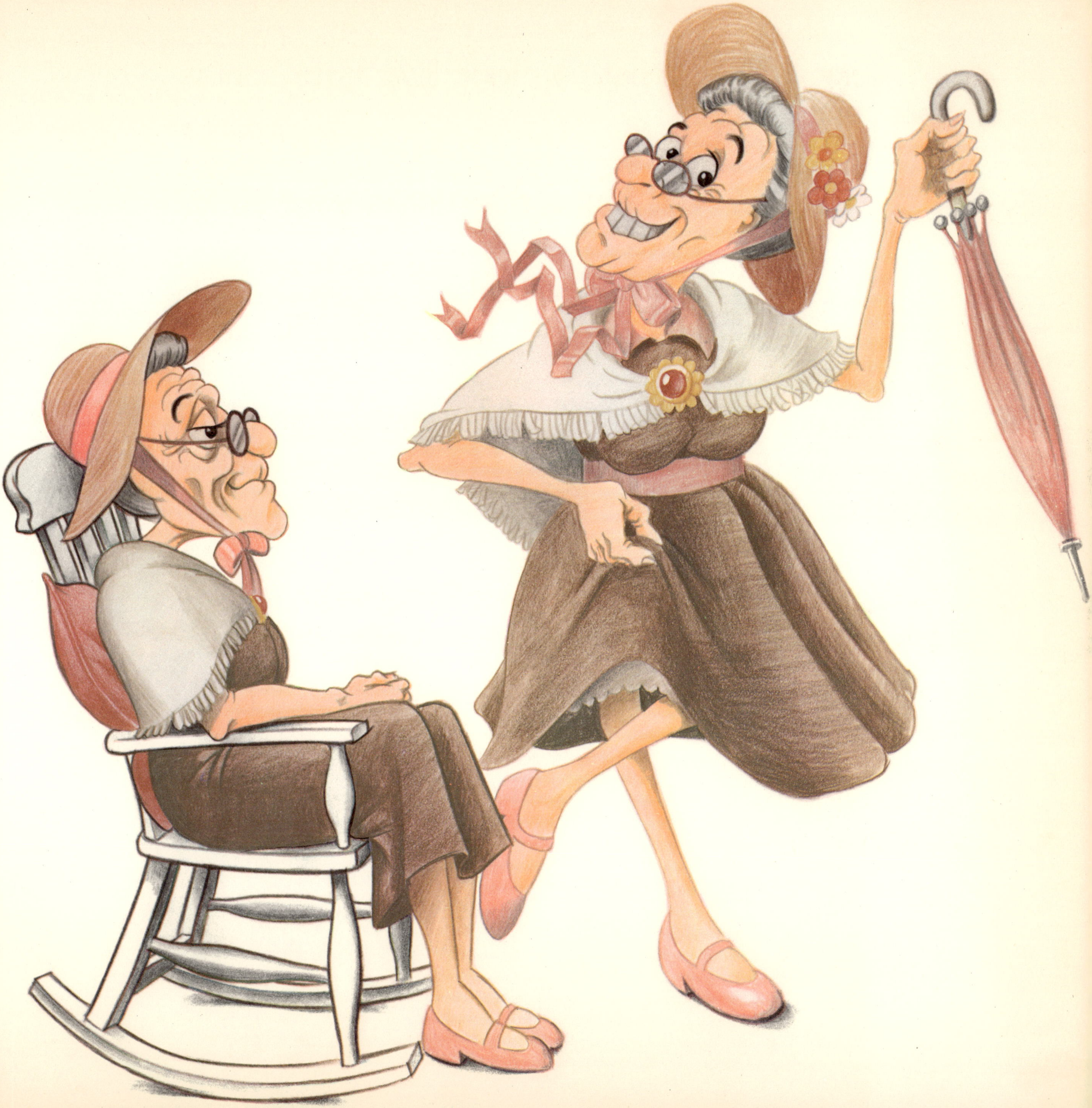

Your body is what you look like. Your soul is what you are.

And the really important difference between your body and your soul is this: unlike your body, your soul doesn't wear out.

An old lady of 90 can still have a very lively soul, even though her body is so old she can hardly climb the stairs any more.

By now, you've probably guessed that when you die, it's only your body that dies. Your soul then begins to go somewhere else.

WHERE'S A GOOD PLACE FOR SOULS TO GO?

As long as there have been people on earth, there have been ideas about where your soul goes after your body has died.

Often, these ideas are very important parts of the different kinds of believing that we call religion. And as there are hundreds of religions, so there are hundreds of ideas about what happens to your soul after death.

For instance, many people, especially in Asia and India, believe that your soul returns to earth after you die, but in a different body. This could be as another person, or as another form of life completely—like a bird or an elephant or even an insect. (This is called reincarnation, and if you believe in it you're very careful about how you treat birds and animals, because you never know when you might be one yourself.)

On the other hand, the American Indians believed that there was one special place where good souls went. It was called the Happy Hunting Grounds.

If you were lucky enough to go there, you would find great herds of buffalo—more than enough for everybody. So there would always be good buffalo steaks to eat, and a thick cloak of buffalo hide to keep you warm.

But suppose you believed in reincarnation, and didn't like the idea of eating buffalo steaks? Or didn't even know what a buffalo was? Then the Happy Hunting Grounds wouldn't be much of a place for your soul to go.

And so we find that all through time, different people have had their own special ideas about the kind of place they would like their souls to go.

The old warrior Vikings, who used to like nothing better than a good fight and plenty to drink afterwards, believed that all brave warriors went to Valhalla. This was a splendid palace with a roof made from shields (large round pieces of armor that Vikings used to protect themselves during sword fights).

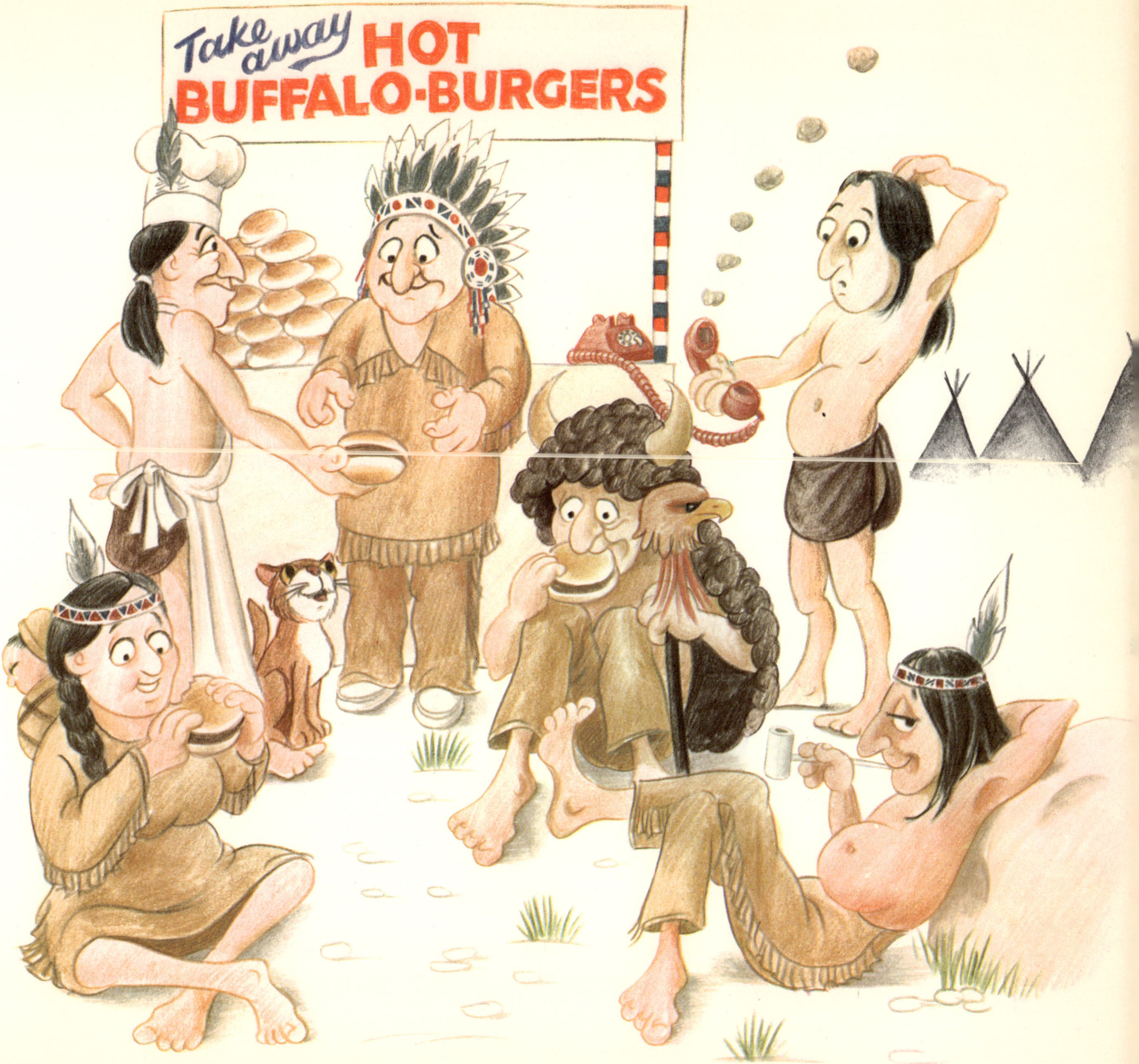
Take away HOT
BUFFALO-BURGERS

There was roast boar to eat, as much as you wanted to drink, and all your old warrior friends to fight with every day. It sounds exhausting, but it was their idea of a wonderful time.

Africans, Indians, Chinese, Russians—just about every race you can think of has had its own special and personal place where souls go after the body has died. For thousands of years, no matter how different people may have been in color or customs or language, they have nearly all believed that there is another kind of life after our life as a person on earth.

(Of course, there are people who don't believe in a life after their life on earth. But if you were ever able to count them, there are many more believers than non-believers.)

Today, although the belief has stayed pretty much the same, you don't hear too many people talk about the Happy Hunting Grounds or Valhalla. Instead, we have Heaven.

But, as a complete opposite, we also have Hell. And now that you have the idea of another life after life on earth, maybe we should pay Hell a short visit.

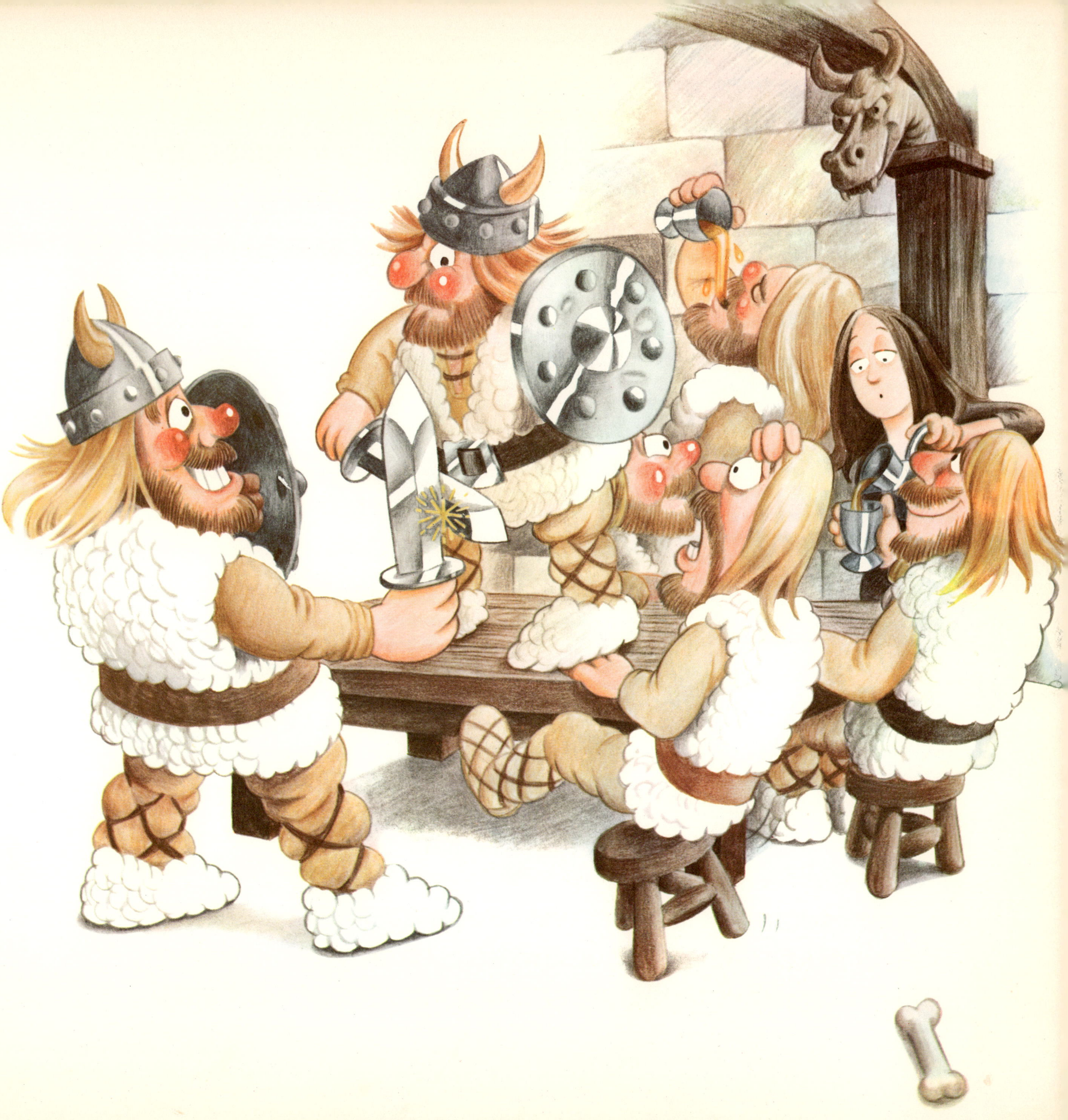

WHAT'S HELL LIKE?

Hell is the worst place you could imagine. But that's probably the way it should be. Because Hell is the place reserved for people who have been really bad during their lives on earth.

Just like Heaven, there have been many ideas through the ages of what Hell is like, and they are all very, very unpleasant.

To show you what we mean, here's just one of the old stories about Hell.

The first bad thing about it is where it is: deep in the middle of the earth. There is no sunshine, no sky, no trees, no laughter, no fun.

And it's hot—hotter than any place on earth. Great fires burn all the time to keep it boiling hot. In fact, it's so hot that even the rocks burn, and very bad-smelling stuff called brimstone comes bubbling out of them.

You almost feel sorry for souls who have gone to Hell, no matter how wicked they've been. They're always thirsty, but never allowed to drink. And they

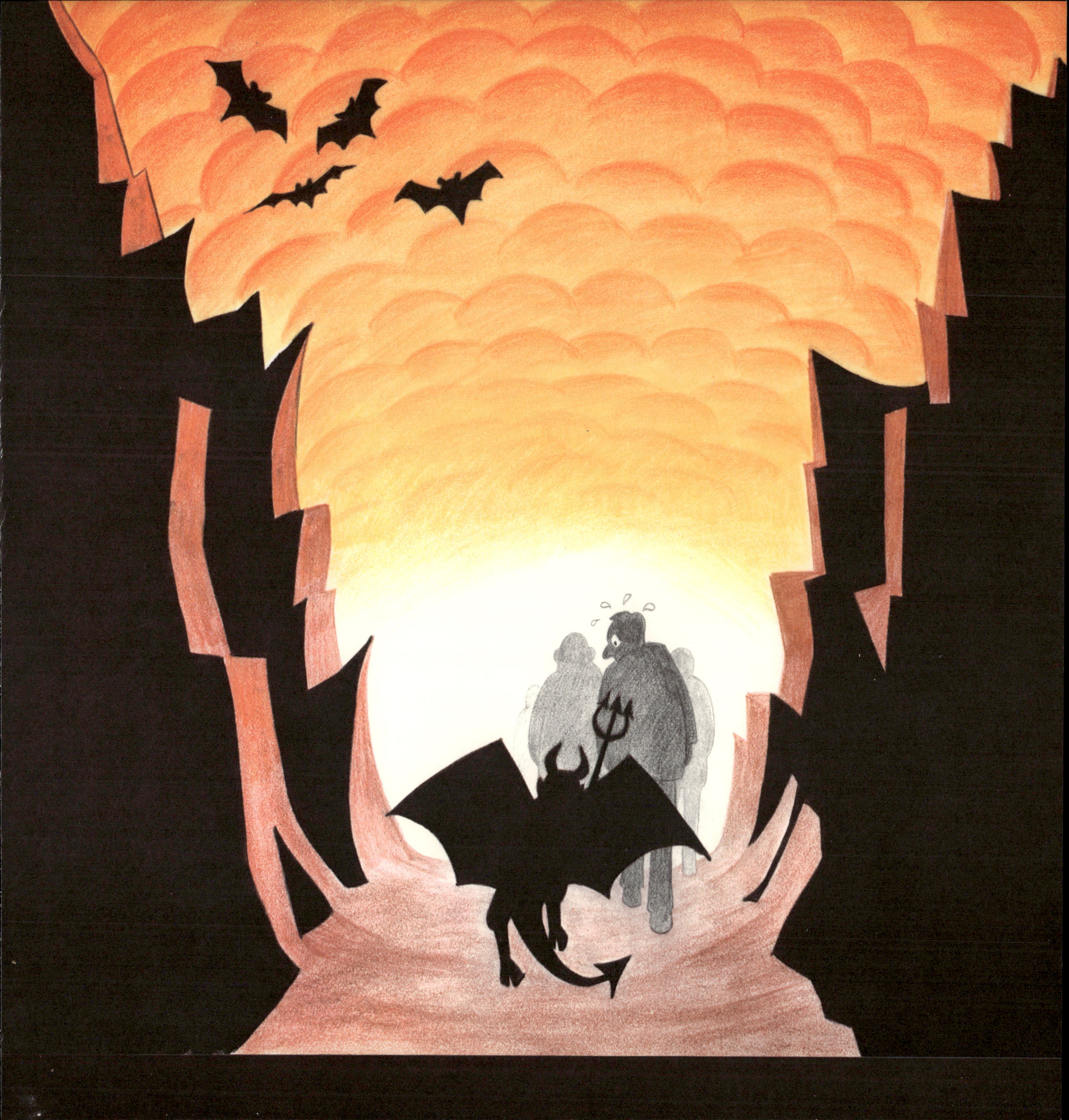

have to work very hard stoking up the fires, with never a day off.

To make sure they keep on working, Hell has its own kind of government. At the head of it is an evil character called the Devil, and he has a whole army of assistant Devils who help to keep everything going as uncomfortably as possible for all the souls down there.

Old pictures of the Devil show him with hooves (rather like goats have) instead of feet, a long pointed tail, and horns sticking out of his head. His eyes are burning red, and when he breathes, fire and brimstone come out of his mouth. All in all, the kind of figure you'd rather not meet.

He usually carries with him a long three-pronged fork called a trident, which he uses to prod all those souls who aren't working hard enough. And his greatest pleasure is creating unhappiness for others.

That's only one of the ways in which Hell was described in the old days.

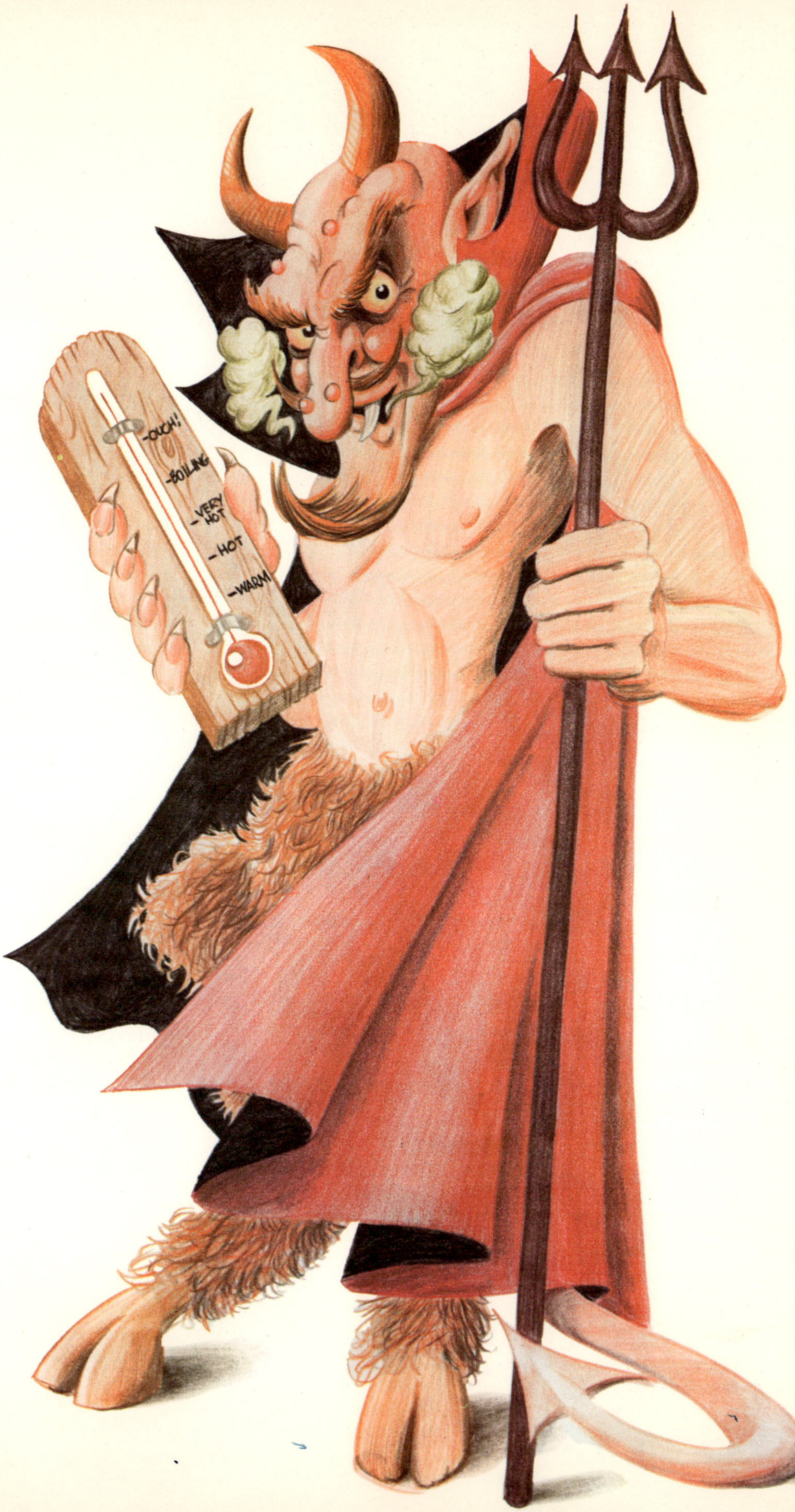
OUCH!
BOILING
VERY HOT
HOT
WARM

But people then were much more simple in their ideas than we are now. Today, we think we know a lot more about everything, and it's old-fashioned to believe in a strange creature who runs around poking people with his trident.

So the old idea of the Devil isn't as common as it once was. The idea of Hell, though, is still very much with us.

It may not be that simple kind of Hell you've just read about, because that's really just a very uncomfortable place for the body.

Hell as we imagine it today is more of an uncomfortable place for the soul.

Perhaps the best way of explaining it is to compare it with something you know about.

Do you remember the last time you were very unhappy?

Not just because you fell down and skinned your knee, but because of something much more serious. Maybe you had a pet that died, or you felt that other people didn't like you, or you were very lonely. Anyway, whatever the reason, you felt really gloomy and miserable, and you felt you were never going to enjoy anything ever again.

Hell must be a little like that; a kind of deep, bad unhappiness that just goes on and on.

Unhappiness, like other feelings, changes from person to person. So it's likely that Hell changes from person to person too, instead of the one kind of Hell that the old stories describe.

But although our ideas about Hell may have changed over the years, our ideas about why souls go there have basically stayed the same. Hell is now, as it always has been, for people who have caused a lot of unhappiness on earth. It's only fair that they get their share of unhappiness too.

Luckily, there's something much better to look forward to: Heaven.

WHAT'S HEAVEN LIKE?

If Hell is our idea of the worst possible place to be, Heaven is the best.

And there have been just as many ideas and descriptions of Heaven as there have been about Hell. This is just one of them.

It starts with the directions for finding Heaven, and they're quite easy. You just go straight up into the sky, through the clouds and there you are.

Facing you, as you come up through the clouds, is a pair of huge gates, sometimes called the Pearly Gates because they're white and shiny. And standing at the gates is a very, very old man.

You might think that this is God, because God is in charge of Heaven just as the Devil is in charge of Hell. In fact, the very old man is not God, but Saint Peter, one of God's chief Angels. (Angels take care of Heaven in the same way that Devils take care of Hell; but Angels are much nicer.)

You go up to the gates and tell Saint Peter who you are; and he looks up your name in a book that he keeps by his side.

Please Wait

This book must be truly enormous, because in it are the names of every person in the world. Not only that. There are also notes on what everybody has done during his or her life on earth, rather like the report cards you get at school.

So everything you've done is in the book. If you've done more bad things than good things, you won't be allowed through the gates. Instead, Saint Peter will turn you away. And it's no good promising to be good if he lets you into Heaven, because by then it's too late. So down to Hell you go.

But if the big book shows that you've led a good life, you're allowed through the gates and into Heaven.

This is where many of the old stories about Heaven stop. Some of them describe Angels sitting among the clouds and playing music on their harps, but there's not very much to tell us what everybody else does all day.

So we thought it might be interesting to imagine what Heaven might be like for four very different souls.

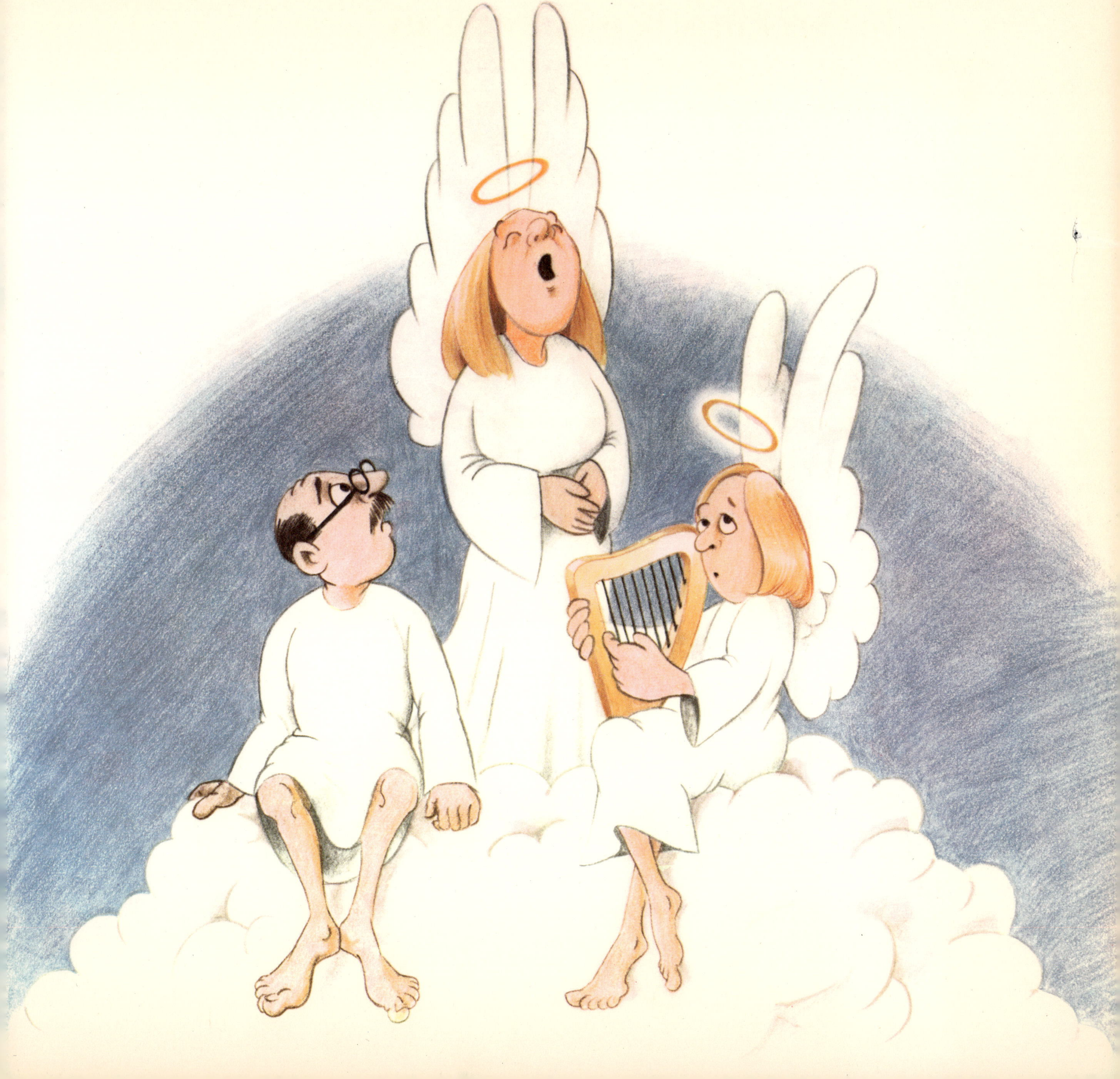

HEAVEN FOR MOTHERS.

Think of the kind of life your Mother has. There's a family to look after, there's a home to look after, and there may be a job to look after as well. She has very little time to herself.

So Heaven for her might be having a little more time, and not so many chores.

Having breakfast in bed, instead of always fixing breakfast for everybody else.

Having a long, relaxed bath, instead of a quick shower.

Going horseback riding, instead of going to the supermarket.

Reading books, instead of doing the dishes.

Going out to the theatre, instead of staying home and watching TV.

These may not sound like very heavenly things to you, because they're not big or exciting. But for all we know, Heaven might be a collection of little things like that. Not a completely different kind of life; just a better kind of life.

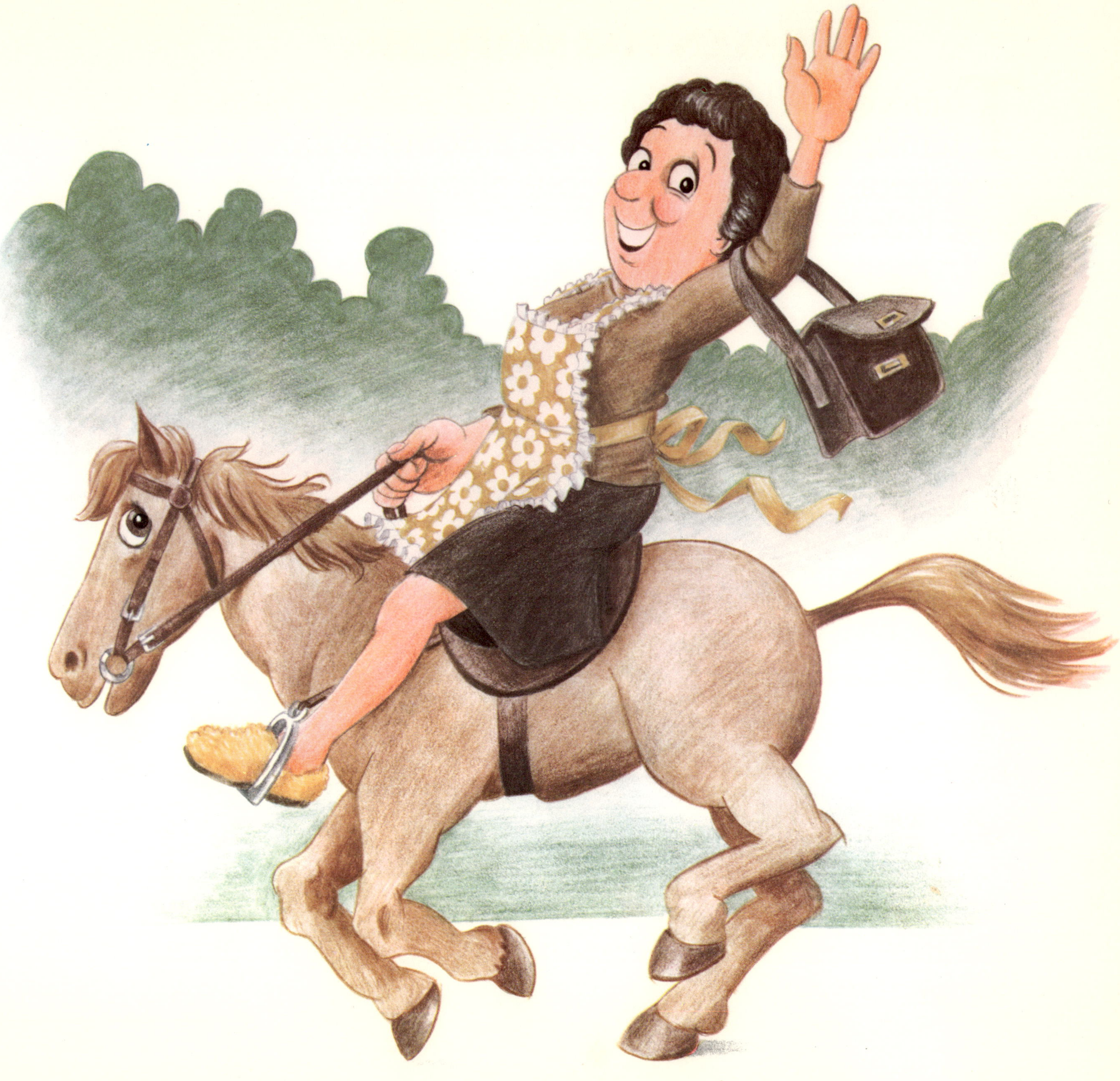

HEAVEN FOR FATHERS.

If you ask your Father, he'll probably tell you that he gets more bills through the mail than just about anybody in the world. And he hates them—doctor bills, garage bills, bills from the TV repair man, bills from the tax man.

In a Heaven for Fathers, bills would be banned. So would early morning meetings, bad-tempered bosses and working weekends.

Saturday mornings, the golf club would be uncrowded; Saturday afternoons, there'd be a great ball game to watch. And Sundays, you'd take him somewhere nice instead of having him take you to the zoo for the 134th time.

More important, even work would be fun. So even Monday mornings would be OK.

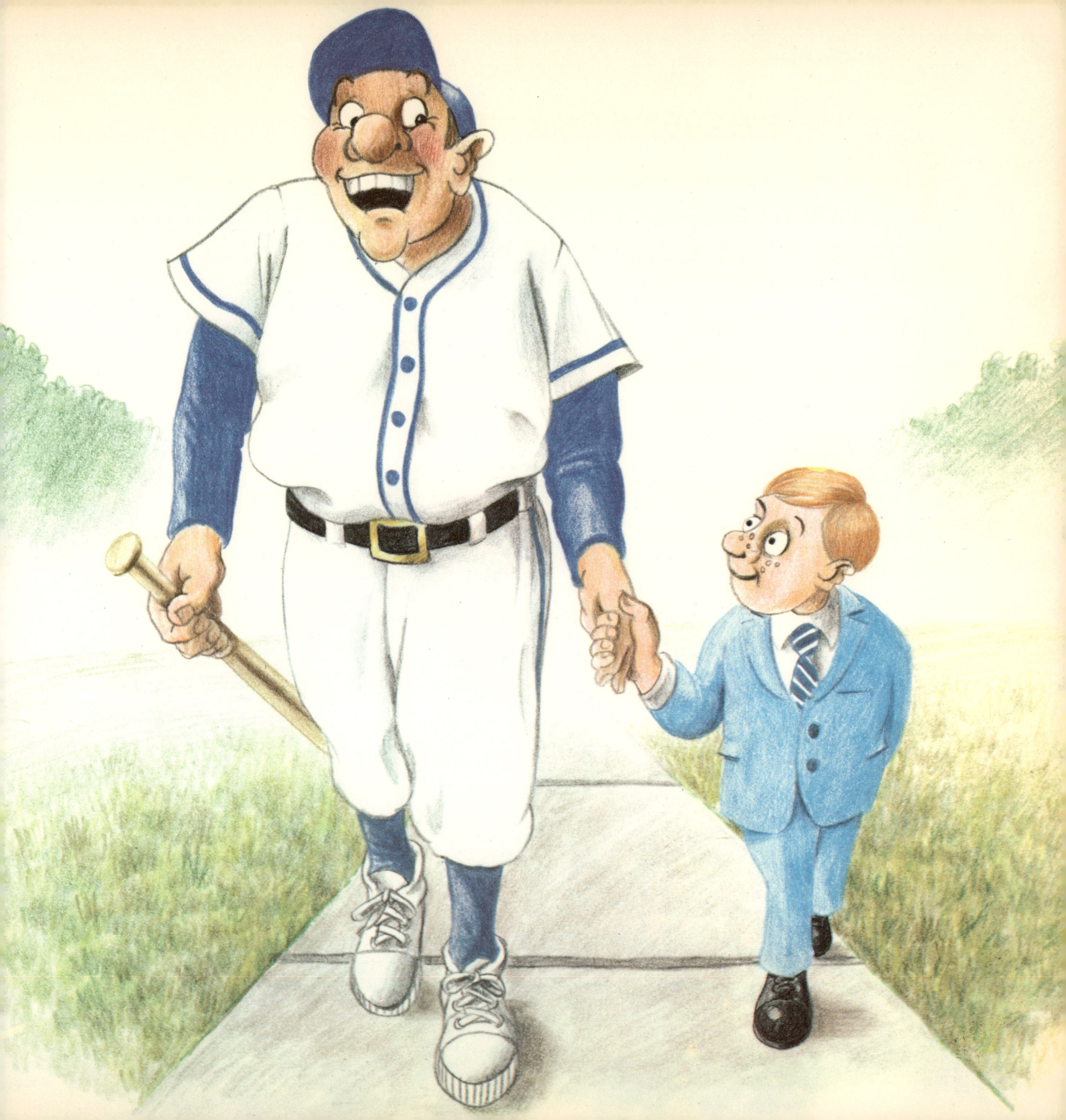

HEAVEN FOR DOGS.

Who says Heaven is just for humans? It might be that every living thing has the same chance as a person does to have a life after life on earth. And that includes your favorite dog.

His idea of Heaven would probably start with trees. (For some reason, dogs love sniffing around trees almost as much as they love sniffing around other dogs.)

Then he'd want plenty of flower beds, where he could bury his bones and get his nose good and muddy.

Maybe a cat or a mailman to bark at and chase every once in a while.

Other dogs, to run with.

And at night, a place in front of the fire to sleep, with someone to tickle his tummy.

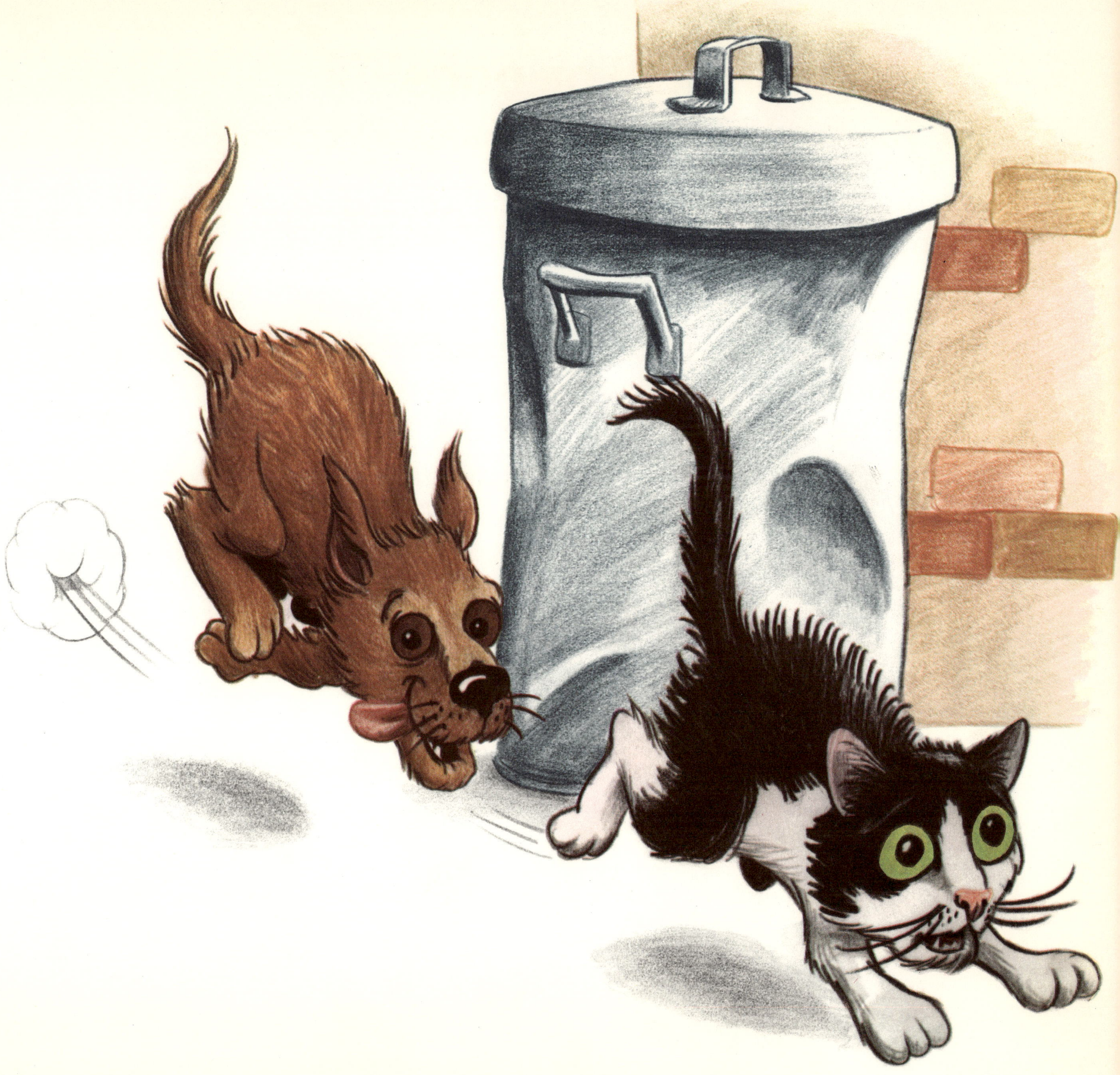

HEAVEN FOR ASTRONAUTS.

If you were an astronaut, think how great it would be to have a space capsule you could walk around in, so you wouldn't have to sit all scrunched up for days on end.

A space capsule that was so big you could have a pool in it, and go swimming on your way to Mars.

And wouldn't it be nice, once you got to Mars, if you didn't have to wear those heavy boots and suits and helmets; and the Martians were really friendly and pleased to see you; and their ice cream was even better than the kind you get at home.

It sounds good, doesn't it? Although if you asked a real astronaut, maybe he'd want something very different in his Heaven.

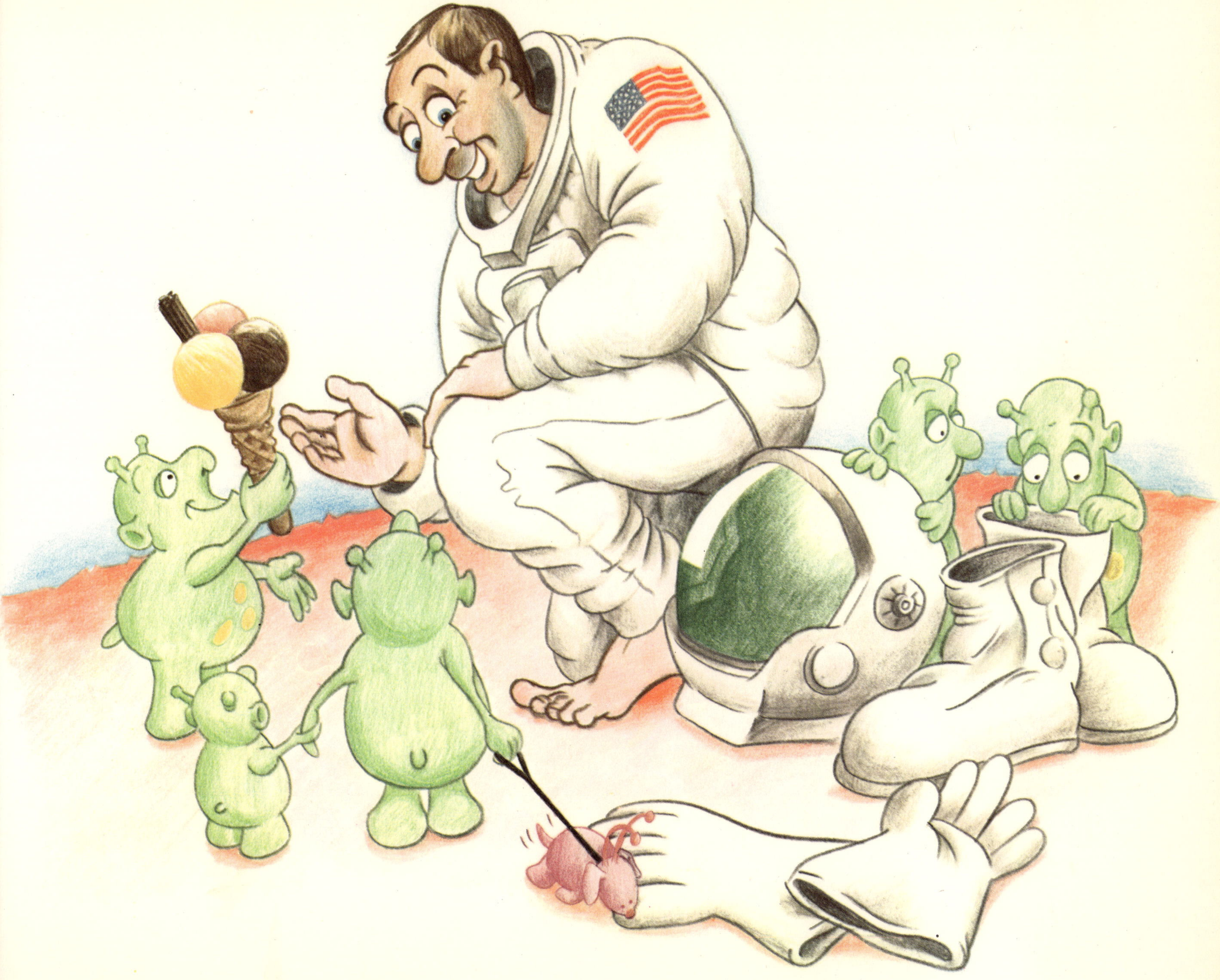

Now, these four ideas about Heaven may not be very good ones, but they do show you what we believe to be a true thing: Heaven is very personal. Your kind of Heaven wouldn't make me happy, and my kind of Heaven wouldn't be good for you. There are probably as many ideas about Heaven as there are people.

The basic idea, though, is always the same. Heaven is a place where you're happy.

Because we've never been there, we try to imagine what it's like by comparing it with life as we know it on earth, but making it better. Maybe it is like that, maybe not. Maybe it's so very different from anything we know that we simply can't imagine it.

Luckily, it's easier to understand how we get to Heaven.

That's partly because getting to Heaven depends on what we do on earth, so we can understand that. And partly because so many good and sensible people over the years have given us advice on how to get there.

HOW DO WE GET TO HEAVEN?

The way some people talk, you'd think that getting to Heaven is a reward given out by grown-ups for good behavior.

"Kids who leave chewing gum under the table don't go to Heaven."

"You'll never get to Heaven if you don't brush your teeth."

"If you don't eat your vegetables, you won't go to Heaven."

It's true that brushing your teeth and eating your food are important. But just because you have clean teeth and a clean plate doesn't mean you go to Heaven. It's not as simple as that.

It's more a question of how you live the whole of your life on earth. As you've just read, many good people over the years have thought about that; and although they lived at different times and in different countries, it's amazing how alike their ideas are.

They're not rules. They're not a list of do's and don'ts. They're simple, common-sense thoughts on how life should be lived.

Being kind.

One of the nicest things you can be is kind, but it's not always easy. You can be kind to someone you like without even thinking. But you can also hurt people without thinking: it's much easier to make people sad than it is to make them happy.

Being kind means thinking about how other people feel, and not just how you feel. And that's hard work. But it's worth it. Because you'll find that if you give kindness to others, they'll give it back to you. It's rather like a marvelous present that never wears out.

Telling the truth.

We all tell lies. Sometimes out of kindness, but more often because we're scared to tell the truth. The trouble about telling lies is that you can never kid yourself. You always know when you've told one, and the more you try to forget it, the more it comes back to bother you.

So in the long run, the person who suffers most when you tell lies is you. Other people will stop believing what you say, and may even stop seeing you because of that. But you can't stop seeing yourself.

There are many reasons for telling the truth, but the best one of all is that it makes you believe in yourself.

Being happy.

If you think about it, you'd rather have happy friends than miserable friends, because happy people are much more fun to be with. They feel the same way about you.

Happy people are never lonely.

There's no short cut to being happy. But there is a way of thinking which most happy people seem to have. They enjoy what they've got, instead of worrying about what they don't have.

Try it. If you think your allowance is too small, think about the kids who never have an allowance. If you'd like a new bicycle, think about kids who are too sick to ride a bike.

You're lucky. You've got a lot to be happy about.

Now, suppose you're already kind and truthful and happy. Is there something else you should do?

Yes there is, and it's very important. You've got to try to be like that all the time, and not only on weekends or when you feel like it.

Then something really good will happen. Because if you're happy, you'll find it will spread to people around you. And when you're surrounded by happiness, you're halfway to Heaven already. Even when you have the rest of a long life ahead of you.

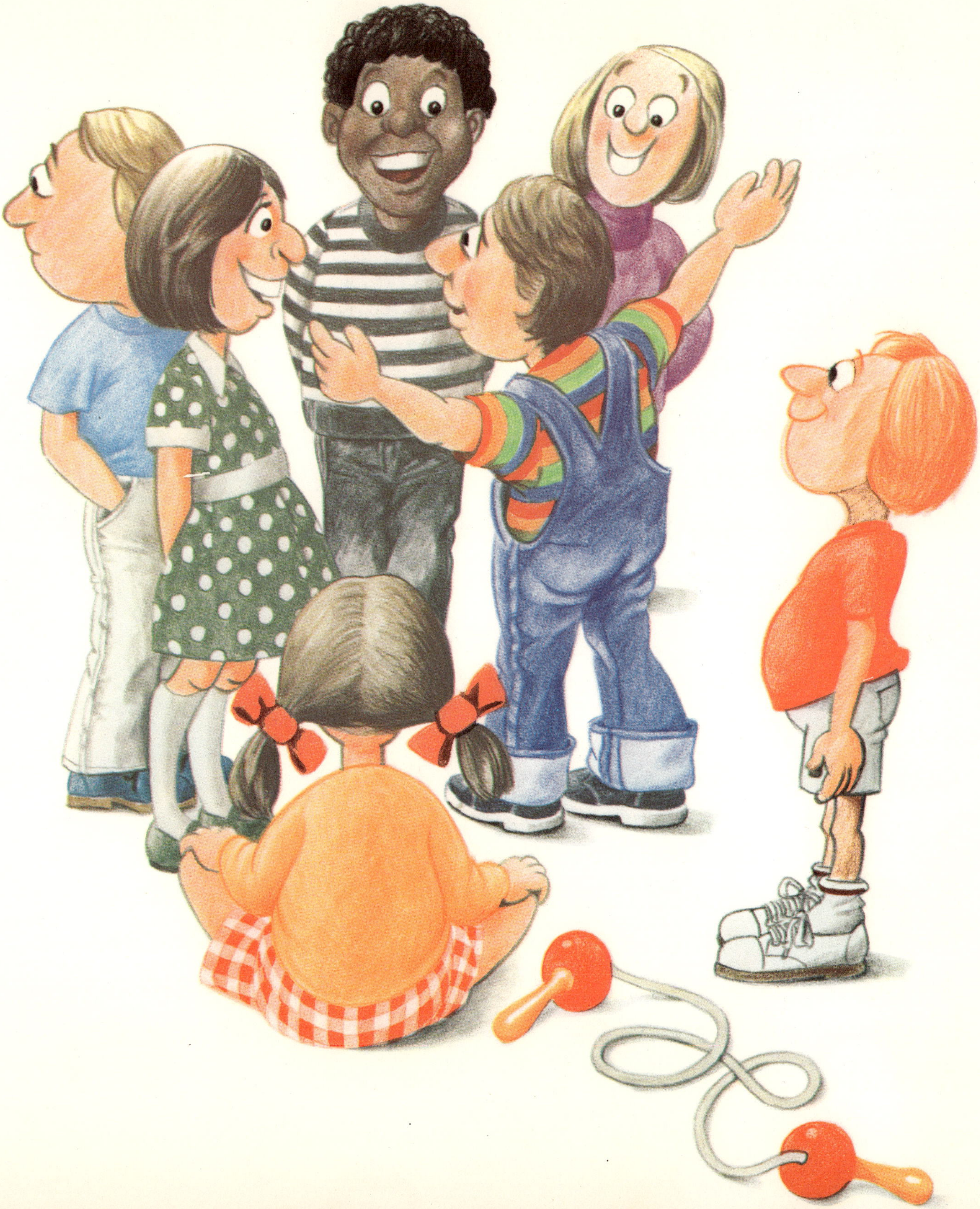

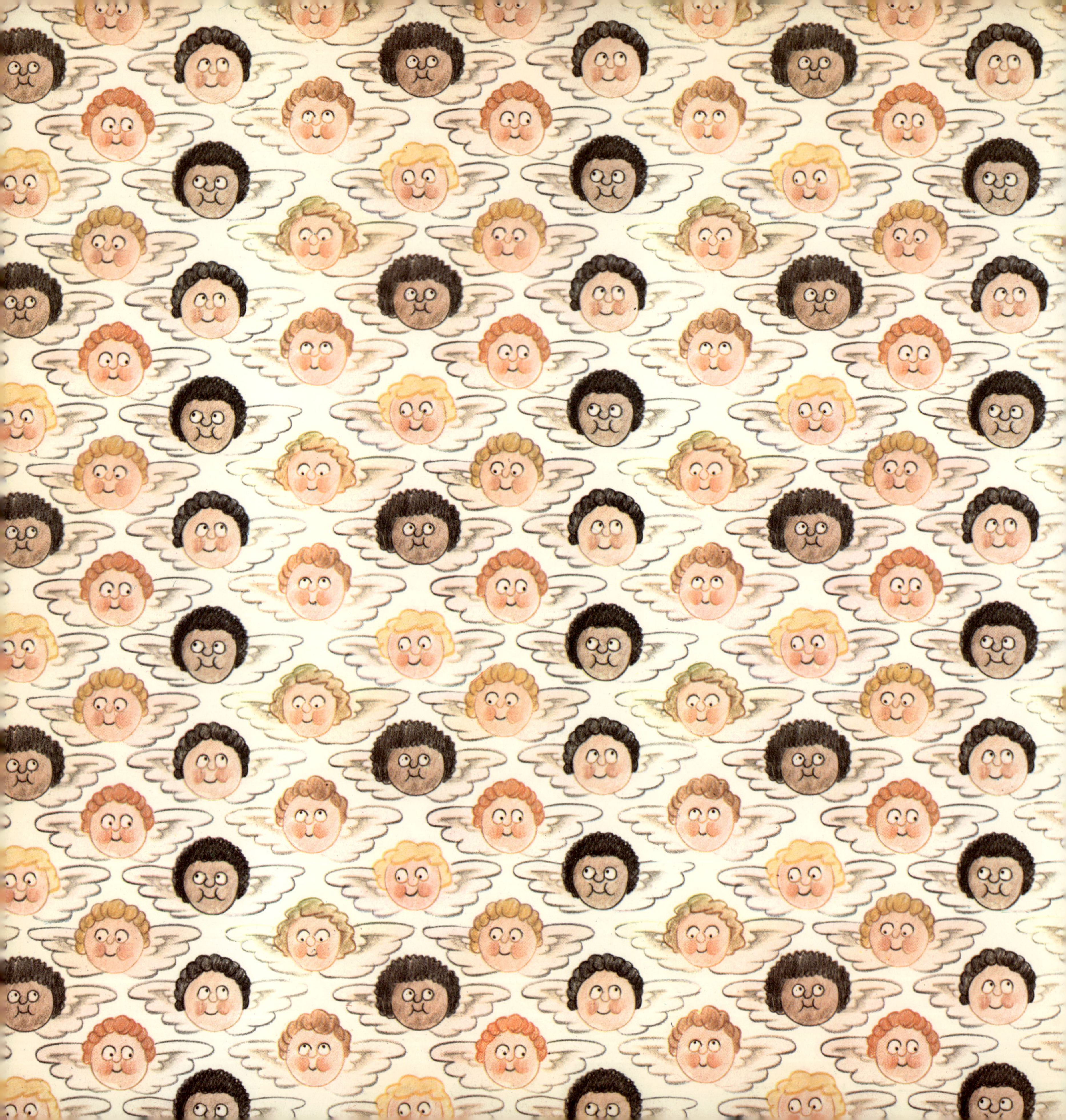